This book was given to

Jim

by

Claude & Wanda

ACKNOWLEDGEMENTS

BRANDT & BRANDT, for "How To Make A Husband A Father" by Shirley Jackson, copyright © 1960 by Shirley Jackson.

THOMAS Y. CROWELL COMPANY, INC., for excerpt from *How To Be A Father* by Frank B. Gilbreth, Jr., copyright © 1958 by Frank B. Gilbreth, Jr., and James J. Spanfeller.

HARPER & ROW PUBLISHERS, INC., for excerpt from *My Ten Years In A Quandary And How They Grew* by Robert Benchley, copyright © 1936 by Robert C. Benchley; for "A Toast To Baby" from "The Babies" in *Mark Twain's Speeches* by Mark Twain, copyright © 1910 by Harper & Row Publishers, Inc., copyright © 1923, 1951 by The Mark Twain Company.

SIMON & SCHUSTER, a Division of Gulf and Western Corporation, for excerpt from *What Dr. Spock Didn't Tell Us* by B.M. Atkinson, Jr., copyright © 1959 by B.M. Atkinson, Jr.

DOUG SPANGLER, for excerpt from the "Frankly For Fathers" column in the July 1977 issue of *American Baby*.

HELLO, DADDY!

So you're going to be a Father!

by *dolli tingle*

with some other highly qualified commentators.

The C. R. Gibson Company
Norwalk, Connecticut

So you're going to be a father!
My, my, isn't that just splendid!
Now you mustn't for a moment
Think your carefree life is ended.
You can always get a sitter
For a fairly hefty fee.
Or, leave dinner in the oven,
WE'LL all come and sit for free!

A Toast To Baby!

. . . We have not all had the good fortune to be ladies. We have not all been generals, or poets, or statesmen; but when the toast works down to the babies, we stand on common ground. . . .

The idea that a *baby* doesn't *amount* to anything! Why, one baby is just a house and a front yard full by itself. *One* baby can furnish more business than you and your whole Interior Department can attend to. He is enterprising, irrepressible, brimful of lawless activities. Do what you please, you can't make him stay on the reservation. Sufficient to the day is one baby. As long as you are in your right mind don't you ever pray for twins. Twins amount to a permanent riot. And there ain't any real difference between triplets and an insurrection. . . .

Mark Twain

Exercises

Feet Muscles

Let's begin at the bottom. It may surprise you to know that strong feet muscles are very important to you as a father. Fatherhood brings many additional loads for you to carry. If your feet aren't up to it, you'll have increasing difficulty along the way. So look to your feet, men.

This exercise will help you with one of the most difficult tasks for a new father: getting out of bed in the middle of the night to comfort or feed a crying baby. First, heel-and-toe-it to your bed and lie down. Relax and get comfortable. Now, swing your feet around and place them firmly on the floor as you sit up in bed. Count to ten and breathe deeply. Place all your weight on your feet as you stand up. Aim yourself toward your baby's room. At the same time say authoritatively, "I'll get it, dear; you go back to sleep." Relax and repeat. I advise you to practice this exercise over and over until it becomes a reflex action. Then when your baby comes, you'll be prepared.

Stretching

Stand with your feet a shoulder-width apart. Reach up with your hands as high as you can. Now bend over and try to touch your toes. Start easy and work up to ten toe touches. Then begin with the same stance, arms over head. Bend backward as far as you can without falling down. Finally, with arms over head, bend to each side as far as you can. Relax and repeat as much as you like.

Research has shown that a stretched father is a happier father. From the beginning, it seems we fathers are always bending over or stretching up to do something. There are play yards to collapse, mobiles to hang, rooms to paint, diapers to change, and baths to give. And there are endless toys to pick up. One father told me that it wasn't until he had children that he understood the Biblical verse, "When I became a man, I put away childish things."

The father who doesn't practice his stretching exercises will soon discover many aches and pains all over his body.   *Doug Spangler*

I understand it won't be long
Before we greet the tad.
Oh, he's sure to be a tiger
Just exactly like his Dad!

A baby is the only case where an addition automatically becomes a deduction.

There's nothing like having a baby to make you realize that it's a changing world.

A new daddy can never understand why most babies have to be born at three o'clock in the morning.

Don't panic when she tips the scales
A little more each day.
The odds are ten to one that she
Won't always look this way.

Naming The Baby

As soon as practicable after the new arrival has been given a welcome reception to the home it should also be given a name. Some parents seem to think the naming of a baby is a matter that can very well wait their leisure and convenience. They ask lightly "What's in a Name?" and thus the christening becomes indefinitely delayed. The author of this work insists that it is more important a baby should have a name than that a grownup should have an appendix or that a dog should have two tails. To start a baby out in life without a name is like sending an express package without any address. In order to preserve its individuality in the world, the baby must be labeled. It must be roped, thrown and branded. It must have a handle by which it may be known among the masses.

Fancy a baby growing up without having its own individual trademark! What would a boy baby sign to his checks when he becomes a man? When, as often happens, a controversy arises in the home over naming Baby, a compromise is effected by giving it a temporary cognomen, but this plan is attended by the gravest risk, because such names frequently stick for life. A man dislikes to grow up with no other name than "No. 2 Smith" or "Cherub," or "Puddin'." No young lady likes to be called "Angel" (especially by those who have no right to call her that) or "Bright-Eyes," or "Roly-Poly." Give the baby a name and tack it on as soon as possible. . . .

In christening do not forget that Baby has some rights in the matter. Do not fasten upon it a name that will make it feel foolish after it grows up. A stalwart man who stands six foot three in his socks is no "Clarence," nor "Claude," nor "Percy." By the same token a tall, angular, stern-visaged Amazonian "New Woman" doesn't fit the name "Angelica," which means "lovely, angelic," or "Laura," which has the significance of "clinging ivy." She'd better by far have the name of "Bridget," which means "strength," or "Ursula," which means "she-bear."

If it's a baby boy and he has a rich old uncle, name the child after the uncle. But even this does not always work out in practice—frequently the uncle leaves all his wealth to charity and the baby doesn't even get honorable mention in his will.

Newton Newkirk

I see what you've been reading
Did you think I wouldn't look?
Well, let me say—
No child of mine
Will ever be named "BOOK"!

I know my wife won't hurry up
She's such a stubborn dame.
And just when I've got tickets
To the All Star Super Game!

At The Hospital

... things must have been easier when people believed in the stork.

My wife has been on a diet for nine months—I've lost ten pounds.

Whoever said that anticipation was half the fun?

My wife drove to the hospital—my pains were too close together.

Have a baby—I just had a cigar.

How To Make A Husband A Father

The new father is a familiar and irresistibly comic figure, for some reason, and his behavior at the arrival of his child is traditionally that of an irrational creature, caught in a situation of infinite confusion and bewilderment. When his wife is ready to leave for the hospital he is expected to run back and forth mindlessly, wholly unable to remember the name of the doctor, the hospital, or his wife. At the hospital (provided he gets there at all, and is not left behind by a wife bent on more practical things) he will pace wildly up and down, catching nurses by the arm, and addressing every white-coated stranger as "Doctor." When he is informed that he has a child he will faint. He will then tiptoe to the bedside of his wife, who is getting a well-deserved sleep after the rough work is over, stumble heavily against the foot of the bed, and announce joyfully to his wife and the nurse that the baby is a boy, or the baby is a girl. After this, leaving an entire, usually perfectly efficient system in ruins behind him, he will rush out to buy football suits, tennis rackets, golf clubs, and enormous toy elephants for his child, who is already the biggest, handsomest, most wide-awake baby in the hospital nursery. He will have a fatuous smile on his face, and he will be unable to stop himself from telling everyone from the bus driver to the lady in the florist shop about his baby. *Shirley Jackson*

You have to get started early
When you know that you've got a champ.
So I've signed the kid up
For the local "Y"
And a session at summer camp.

Bringing
Baby Home

Marriage is the biggest change in a man's life, but the next biggest change is when he and his wife bring home their first baby. Most men recognize both changes as for the better, although at first there may be some gloomy moments when the bride appears in the light of a roommate for a semester that will never end; and the new baby appears in the light of a house guest who will never go away.

Naturally, the new father's living habits and status around the house will change when the baby is brought home. Almost everything that the father does—how loud he plays television, how much hot water he uses, what time he wakes up in the morning, when he eats his meals—is governed by the demands of the baby. And the house can never be left unmanned for a single moment, unless the baby is removed from it as well.

Up to the arrival of his first baby, the average male has never experienced a recurring night-time disturbance that he could neither remedy nor move his residence away from. In the past, when any noise had disturbed his slumber, he had shouted a complaint, rapped on the ceiling, telephoned the police, turned the noise off, put it outside, thrown shoes at it, or taken some other sort of satisfying concrete action. Indeed, he had considered such action not only his personal right but his civic duty.

And now, for the first time, he finds in the baby's crying a frustrating kind of disturbance that he can't sleep through, can't move away from, and can't stop by complaints, threats, or throwing shoes. He knows very well that violence of any sort or raucous protests would intensify rather than alleviate the disturbance. And he learns quickly that the disturbance can best be terminated by the exact opposite of violence, which is gentleness.

So, after a lifetime of sound sleep, the father must not only grow accustomed to broken sleep but must discipline himself to greet the unwelcome awakenings with whispered sweet talk and lullabies, rather than coarse shouts and curses.   *Frank Gilbreth, Jr.*

Holding The Baby

No male relative, in his right mind, ever takes a baby to hold of his own free will. The very thought of dropping it, a thought which is always present, is enough to reduce all his vital organs to gelatin. Some female always suggests it. "Let Joe hold him for a minute. Hold him, Joe!"

So, Joe, sweating profusely, picks the infant up and becomes a figure of fun. "Look at how Joe's holding him, Bessie! Like he was a golf bag!" "Poor kid—put him down, Joe!" "Look out, Joe, you'll strangle him!" Lynching is in the air.

But now Joe can come back with the excuse that he is giving the baby exercise. "You women hold him in that one position all the time, and his body doesn't develop symmetrically. Ask anyone who knows!"

For male relatives who find it necessary to hold a baby, the following positions are suggested as being most beneficial to the child's development and most conducive to apprehension on the mother's part.

If the child has to be lifted from its crib by the father or uncle, the old-fashioned way of reaching down and grabbing it under the arms should be discarded. The male relative should get into the crib with the child, and lie on his back (his own back), taking the child on his chest and rising to a sitting posture. Then call for someone else to come and lift both father and child from the crib at once.

In taking the baby from the arms of someone else, as at the christening or general family gathering, grasp one of the child's ankles firmly in the right hand and tell the other person to let go. The child will then swing, head down, from the other person's arms, and can be twirled in a semicircle, and in the manner of an adagio dancer, until the arc is completed, and the child lands across the uncle's shoulder, the latter, if possible, still holding firmly onto the ankle. This will develop the child's leg, and give it poise.

For just ordinary holding, a good bit of exercise can be worked into a method whereby the male relative holds the child by both wrists and lets it hang down in front of him, swinging slowly back and forth like a pendulum. It can then be tossed high into the air and caught, or not, as Fate will have it.

A still better way to develop the child is to have it hold the male relative.   *Robert Benchley*

A father can't help showing pride
When taking baby for a ride.
He knows they make a handsome pair
While going out to get the air.

But what he always hopes for most
Is meeting friends so he can boast.

The nicest thing about being a baby is that everything you do is wonderful.

Unknown

All babies look alike. That is, all other people's babies.

Unknown

Teach your child to hold his tongue, he'll learn fast enough to speak.

Benjamin Franklin

Revere's Visitation

A temporary form of insanity in which the baby will place himself on all fours somewhat in the manner of a jockey astride a horse and then will commence to ride this imaginary horse as though he is aboard a Kentucky Derby winner. The rocking of the crib can be heard throughout the house and quite often in the next block. Upon first hearing this noise, a new father immediately assumes that at least eight burglars are breaking into the house. Especially is this true if the child suffers a seizure between midnight and 4:00 A.M. Technically the disease at this hour is known as REVERE'S VISITATION.

Goat Mouth

A dietary phenomenon in which babies, usually from nine to twenty-four months, are possessed of a great appetite for everything but food, showing a marked preference for coffee grounds, egg shells, lamp cords, soap, soil, crib railings, dog biscuit and quite often the ear of the dog itself. Just how the infant, with his small and limited number of teeth, can chew his way through crib railings, spaniel ears, etc., will forever remain a mystery to the parent *unless* in an effort to remove splinters, dog hair, egg shells, etc., the parent is stupid enough to stick a finger in said infant's mouth. Not all nine-fingered fathers have power saws.

Miser's Burp

A hardening of the head and heart in which a baby, whose mother is trying to burp him at two o'clock in the morning, will ignore all her patting and pleading and fiendishly refuse to part with the bubble of gas in his stomach that would then permit the poor, groggy woman to deposit him in his crib and stagger back to bed. Fathers caught up in the same situation must exercise the greatest of self-control, as there will be a growing temptation to help the bubble along by gently dangling the little ingrate by his heels.

B. M. Atkinson, Jr.

But after all is said and done
You know you're pleased
To be the one
Who henceforth will be known as Dad.

Being a father is not all bad.

CONGRATULATIONS!

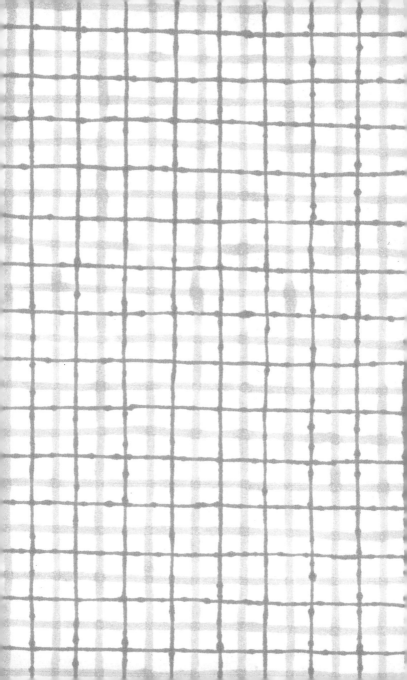